For Her Royal Highness

Princess **Violet**

From

Parker and Sawyer

Presented on the Occasion of:

Your 1st birthday

Princess Tea Parties

Written and Illustrated by **Michal Sparks**

HARVEST HOUSE PUBLISHERS

EUGENE, OREGON

Princess Tea Parties

Text and Artwork Copyright © 2008 by Michal Sparks
Published by Harvest House Publishers
Eugene, OR 97402
www.harvesthousepublishers.com

ISBN-13: 978-0-7369-2276-0
ISBN-10: 0-7369-2276-8

Mr. Gifford B. Bowne II
Indigo Gate
1 Pegasus Drive
Colts Neck, New Jersey 07722

Design and production by Garborg Design Works, Savage, Minnesota

Edited by Janna Walkup

Printed in China

08 09 10 11 12 13 14 / LP / 10 9 8 7 6 5 4 3 2 1

Contents

Each cup of tea represents an imaginary voyage.

Catherine Douzel

Getting Started

Tea parties and princesses—these go together better than almost anything you can think of. After all, it's been said that all girls are princesses. And everyone knows how much fun a tea party can be!

So let's prepare our hearts and our tables for all sorts of tea parties fit for princesses just like you and your friends. Some of these tea parties are very fancy affairs to which you wear beautiful hats and dresses. Sometimes they are simple, spur-of-the-moment get-togethers with a friend or two. But no matter what type of tea party you're hosting, three things are absolutely necessary for a successful gathering—your best manners, a kind heart, and a great big smile.

Before we get started with our planning, let's take a minute to learn a bit about tea.

Did you know that tea has been around for more than five thousand years? The story of how tea came to be is really quite simple. An ancient Chinese emperor liked to drink his water boiling hot. One day a leaf blew into his cup and turned the water brown. The emperor was so thirsty he drank it anyway. And he loved it! In fact, he was so pleased with the taste that he declared that *everyone* should enjoy his new drink. And so tea was born.

The English eventually took tea to another level, transforming it from a simple hot drink into an afternoon event complete with delicious cookies, tempting cakes, and special sandwiches. To the English, "tea" is an ordinary afternoon ritual consisting of a simple snack and a cup of hot tea. "High tea," however, is a fancy afternoon event with an elaborate menu, decorative place settings, and formal dress.

How Do You Take Your Tea?

Tea is made from leaves, but not just any leaves—special tea leaves from certain plants. Some tea is made from the leaves of herbs like peppermint, cinnamon, and chamomile (a tiny, fragrant flower that looks a lot like a daisy).

Tea can also be made from fruits and berries. Have you ever had peach tea? Or perhaps raspberry tea? How about apple spice tea? In the southern part of the United States, people drink "sweet tea"—iced tea with lots of sugar.

Tea can be packaged several different ways. "Loose tea" refers to the dried tea leaves themselves, sometimes mixed with spices, dried fruit, or herbs. When you're fixing this type of tea, you'll need to use a strainer. You can also fix a cup of tea using a "tea bag." The leaves are packaged in a thin paper bag that you simply drop into your teacup or teapot. The bag works as a built-in strainer. Finally, tea is also available as "instant tea." This tea is processed so you can just spoon it into your glass and stir it up. Instant tea is an excellent choice when you want a quick glass of iced tea.

Warm and Cozy Hot Tea

Ready for a cup of hot tea to warm you inside and out on a cold day? First, you'll need to boil the water. (Be sure to have an adult help you with this step.) Fill a teakettle and heat it on the stove until the water boils. Many tea kettles have built-in whistles that let you know when the water boils. While you are waiting for the kettle's whistle, pour some hot water from the sink into your teapot, swirl it around, and then pour it out. This will warm up your teapot.

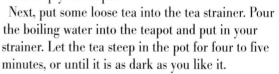

Next, put some loose tea into the tea strainer. Pour the boiling water into the teapot and put in your strainer. Let the tea steep in the pot for four to five minutes, or until it is as dark as you like it.

When you pour tea into your guests' cups, use another strainer to catch any loose tea that may have escaped from the strainer into the teapot.

Cool and Refreshing Iced Tea

Sunny days and soaring temperatures call for a chilly glass of iced tea. Prepare iced tea just as you would hot tea, but let it steep much longer and let it cool to just warm. When it is ready, pour the tea into a tall glass or pitcher filled with ice. The ice will melt, cooling and diluting the tea. Add a lemon wedge or a spoon or two of sugar to taste, stir it up, and enjoy!

Mix It Up!

Once you've mastered the art of making basic hot or iced tea, you can get a bit creative. Add a little apple juice to hot or cold tea for additional flavor and sweetness. Try a traditional slice of lemon or a mint leaf, or experiment with a wedge of peach, some raspberries, or even some blackberries. Or you could get really imaginative and add a splash of lemon-lime soda to a glass of iced tea for a little fizz. Go ahead and be your own tea designer.

Teatime Tools

- *Teakettle*—This is what you boil the water in. It is often made of metal and usually sits on your stove top.

- *Teapot*—This is the pretty container, usually made of ceramic, that often matches your dishes. You pour boiling water into the teapot and then add the tea. A teapot sits on your tea table, and you use it to serve tea to your guests.

- *Tea Strainer*—This is the mesh cup that holds loose tea and allows boiling water to reach the tea but keeps the leaves from floating all over the pot. Some small tea strainers come in fun shapes like pineapples and tiny teapots! These smaller strainers are usually used in a single teacup instead of in an entire teapot.

- *Steeping*—This is the process of the tea soaking into the water. The water becomes darker in color as the tea steeps longer.

1.

A Royal Princess Tea

Our sunny afternoon celebration, medieval princess style, is made complete with brightly colored banners waving in the breeze and a beautiful tent with piles of pillows arranged around a low table, ready and waiting for a regal party of young princesses.

This tea party looks back to the princesses of history who might have spent their own sunshine-filled girlhood afternoons taking tea under a fancy canopy.

You're Invited

For a fun invitation that sets the stage for your tea party, you will need brightly colored construction paper, glitter, some 4-inch squares of tissue paper, scissors, and glue. First, cut out an 8" x 6" piece of construction paper. Fold the paper in half so that the card measures 4" x 6". Then cut a tall triangle with the tall side as the fold. Open up the card and fill in the party information: date, time, place, and your name and phone number. Be sure to ask your guests to RSVP. This stands for *respondez, s'il vous plait,* which is French for, "Please respond so I will know if you can come." Also, let your friends know that the tea party will be held outside.

Now for the decorating! Swirl the glue on the front of the card in a fun pattern and sprinkle on some glitter. Finally, glue one corner of the tissue paper square to the front tip of the cone. Now you have a medieval hat invitation!

Delighful Decorations

For a special touch, use a canopy tent (available in home improvement centers) that you can decorate with extra fabric—no sewing necessary! Just purchase approximately 7 yards of brightly colored fabric and cut it in half down the entire length with scissors or shears (have an adult help with the cutting). Cross the fabric diagonally across the top of the canopy and tie to the legs with ribbons, leaving the end of the fabric loose to blow in the breeze (see illustration).

decorate an umbrella

A round, freestanding umbrella also works well. Simply decorate it with flowing draped fabric and colorful ribbons.

To make light and airy tissue paper banners, you will need a pack of multi-colored tissue paper, a roll of ⅜-inch ribbon, scissors, and a stapler. Fold sheets of tissue paper in half and cut them into a triangle, keeping the fold on the opposite side of the point. Slip the ribbon between the triangles and staple the tissue to the ribbon.

Creative Crafts

• *Great Garlands*—Any medieval princess would love to wear a beautiful garland of ribbons! To make the garland, you'll need wire, silk flowers with long stems (perhaps choosing a different type of flower for each of your friends), and lots of beautiful ribbon. Form a circle with wire to fit the shape of each girl's head, and begin wrapping the silk flowers on the wire using the wire you started with (see illustration). When the flowers are wrapped securely, fold the wire in so it won't poke you. Now, wind the ribbons around the garland to hide the wire. Make sure the ribbons hang nice and long so they flutter when you walk!

• *A Perfect Princess Hat*—Your guests would also feel like royalty wearing traditional princess hats. To construct these, you will need poster board, a stapler, scissors, glue, glitter, braid, jewels, other decorations, and 12-inch squares of tissue paper. First, form the poster board into a cone shape that fits each girl's head. Figure out where the center tip of the hat will be, and then staple one corner of tissue paper on the inside. Next, staple the hat into a cone shape. Finally, decorate the hat to your heart's content!

The Tea Table

A brightly colored tablecloth really adds a festive touch to this tea party. If you don't already have a colorful tablecloth, you can use a piece of fabric instead. Then, take a bunch of ribbons and cut them into little 1-inch squares. Sprinkle the ribbon pieces all over the table—just like confetti! Set a pretty teacup and plate at each place setting along with a colored napkin wrapped with a silk flower. Tie a tag with each friend's name on each flower stem as a cheery place card.

A Mouthwatering Menu

- *Mini Tournament Banner and Crest "Pizzas"*— Spread flavored cream cheese (strawberry is delicious—and pink!) on pieces of toast that have been cut into crest or banner shapes, then make decorations—stripes, dots, swirls, etc.—by squeezing grape jelly through a pastry bag.

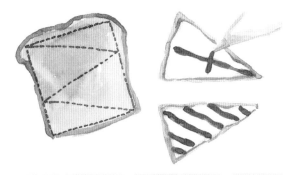

- *Fancy Fruit Salad*—Serve fruit cocktail in tall iced tea glasses along with long iced tea spoons. Easy to prepare and lovely in presentation!

- *Mini Chocolate Cupcakes*— Decorate these time-tested treats with banners, crests, and crowns that have been adhered to toothpicks.

- *Royal Tea*—Decaffeinated Earl Grey served with milk and sugar is delicious. For a sweeter option, serve raspberry or cranberry juice in fancy teacups.

Giggles and Games

- *Hair Braiding with Ribbons*—Braid each other's hair, and then pin and tie with ribbons. This is an especially good activity for older princesses—or try it on your dolls!

- *Crown Ring Toss*—Toss flower garlands onto a miniature maypole.

- *Castle Crests*—Design a crest on heavyweight cardboard and adorn with jewels and glitter. Then glue pin backs on the back for a beautiful royal brooch.

- *Treasure Hunt*—Dress up in princess dresses—from your dress-up stash or simply tied-on fabric capes or skirts—and prepare to find your kingdom's treasure! Mom can hide jewels ahead of time all around the house, and you and your guests can search for them when everyone arrives.

- *Princess Bingo*—Cover a bingo card with jewels as you discover "I spy" items around the house.

2.

A Fairy-Tale Princess Tea

All girls have a favorite fairy-tale princess. Is yours kind Cinderella or trusting Snow White? Perhaps compassionate Belle or Ariel the dreamer? This tea party is all about using your imagination and being the author of your own story. All you need to begin is a cup of tea and a story shared with friends. You already know the beginning: *Once upon a time…*

You're Invited

Let your friends read all about your upcoming event by making your invitations look like a book! You will need brown construction paper, ribbon, a gold paint pen, plain white paper, scissors, tape, and a stapler. Cut the construction paper to 8" x 6" and fold it in half so your card measures 4" x 6". Cut a piece of ribbon almost 5" long and tape it to the inside fold of the brown paper. Then cut the white paper to 7½ x 5½ inches so that it is a bit smaller than the brown paper, fold it in half, and slip it inside the brown paper and over the ribbon. Open the book and staple the spine twice, being careful not to staple the ribbon. Use the gold pen to print the "title" of the book—*A Fairy-Tale Princess Tea Party*—on the front cover. Use the inside pages to record your party information—date, time, place, your name, and phone number.

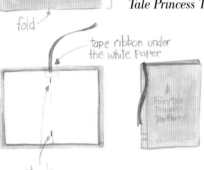

fold

tape ribbon under the white paper

staple

A Fairy-tale Princess Tea Party

Delightful Decorations

Think of all the fairy tales you've heard. What do so many have in common? How about a frog, a crown, a rose, a glass slipper, an apple, or a mirror? Trace these shapes onto plain paper the size of a place mat (approximately 12" x 10"). Color the shapes with markers or crayons. You can even get them laminated at an office supply store or copy shop.

Creative Crafts

Sometimes it's hard to get started writing a story—even a fairy tale! Here's a little help. To create your book, you'll need plain white paper (lined paper is also helpful), pencils, ribbon, a gold pen, construction paper, tape, and a stapler. The cover should be made like the invitation. For illustrations, you'll need colored pencils, markers, stickers, or crayons. First, make the inside pages by creating funny, fill-in-the-blank sentences with a sentence or two on each page—up to 11 pages. Make the books just like you made the invitations, adding three folded pages together instead of one. These can be created ahead of time and handed out at your party. Happy storytelling!

The Tea Table

A pretty white tablecloth makes a nice background for your colorful princess placemats. To get your friends in the writing mood, set a little notebook—open to the first page—at each plate, with your friend's name written on it. (This is the place card!) Tie a sharpened pencil to each napkin with a pretty ribbon. Now, you're ready to start your story!

A Mouthwatering Menu

Of course, writers always need yummy treats to keep the creative thoughts coming.

• *Cinderella's "Broomsticks"*—Use puff pastry (found in the freezer section of the grocery store) and cut into strips, making them thicker at one end. Cut little slices at the thicker end to form the broom's bristles and bake as directed. Dip your broomsticks in ranch dressing for a crunchy and savory treat.

• *Snow White's Apple*—For a unique treat that's just fine to eat, use a mandolin slicer (have an adult help with this) to slice an apple into cross sections.

Make sandwiches—using the apple slices as your bread—with peanut butter and cream cheese.

- *Spice Cake Castle*— Bake a spice cake mix in a sheet cake pan. When the cake is cool, cut it into small rectangles and place the rectangles all around the edges of a round cake plate. Add a layer of frosting with a pastry bag—this is your cement—and stagger the next layer as if the cake rectangles were bricks. Continue moving the "bricks" inward slightly with each layer. When you finish using all your bricks, use yellow icing in a pastry bag to make a "braid" hanging down the side like Rapunzel's hair. If you are a Sleeping Beauty fan, you can use green icing in the pastry bag to create vines that climb up the castle walls!

- *Spicy Tea*—Serve orange or apple spice tea, and stir in a sweet spoonful of honey.

Giggles and Games

- *A Fairy-Tale Performance*—Decide on a fairy tale to act out. You can hand out scripts and assign parts as the guests arrive. Allow enough time to make costumes from a box of dress-up clothes, ribbons, and hats. (You can find great stuff at thrift shops.) Then allow some time for a rehearsal. Put on your performance, complete with lots of drama and laughter.

- *Clay Characters*—Use polymer clay that you bake in the oven to fashion funny characters and props from your favorite fairy tale—a frog with a crown, a ball gown, a pumpkin, a mouse, etc. This clay takes just minutes to bake and your creations will be fun take-home party favors.

- *Movie Time*—Gather around to watch *Ever After* starring Drew Barrymore. This version is visually beautiful, promotes a strong girl character, and even includes entertaining history about Leonardo da Vinci's inventions!

- *Scrapbook Story*—Ask your guests to bring photos of themselves, family, and friends, and put together funny fairy-tale mini scrapbooks using stickers to tell their story. You can find scrapbooking supplies at any arts and crafts or discount department store.

3.

A Princess Tea for Two

Sometimes the very best teatime is a party for two! This could be you and a special friend, your mom, grandma, aunt, or even your dad. Maybe even your brother would like to join you for a spot of tea! This special party can be held in your room, the playroom, the kitchen, or outside. Just think *fun*.

You're Invited

Invitations to this tea party can be as fancy or as simple as you like, but be sure to say something fun like *Have tea with me!* The message can be written on a chalkboard or on a fancy doily, or maybe you can just make a very sweet and polite phone call.

Delightful Decorations

Think balloons! Tie them to the table and the backs of chairs, or just float them around the room. Use a large sheet of white butcher paper for a table-cloth, and draw big teacups on the paper for place mats. Have fun embellishing the teacups—add some polka dots and stripes or flowers. You could even fold paper napkins into silly hats.

Creative Crafts

- *Beautiful Beads*—Using polymer clay that you bake in the oven, make beads that can be sliced with a flower in the center (see illustration). After baking the beads, string them on thin, stretchy elastic to make bracelets, necklaces, and anklets.

- *Design-a-Frame*—This is a special memory maker that's fabulous to do with a parent or grandparent.  Decorate simple cardboard frames with buttons, shells, ribbon, wrapping paper, or items found together on a special nature walk. Then put an extra-special picture—perhaps of you and your guest—in your one of a kind frame!

- *Photo Album Scrapbook*—Mini photo albums are quick and easy to put together, and they help you remember a special time. Use stickers and markers to add fun to the photos.

The Tea Table

Place large sheets of butcher paper on the table. Get out markers, stickers, stamps, and colored pencils and have fun drawing, writing each other messages, playing tic-tac-toe, and other activities. You can even draw your own place settings on the paper. This is easy to set up and a breeze to clean up!

A Mouthwatering Menu

- *Toasted Cheese Sandwiches*—Everyone loves this simple snack! Make toasted cheese sandwiches, and then cut them into long strips and arrange on a pretty cake plate.

- *Ice-Cream Tea*—Place a scoop or two of vanilla ice cream in each pretty china teacup. Fill the matching creamer with chocolate sauce and fill the sugar bowl with sprinkles. When you serve the "tea," ask your guest if she would like chocolate or sprinkles. Garnish the saucers with strawberry slices.

- *Sweet Tea*—Serve chocolate mint tea with cream and sugar. Delicious!

Giggles and Games

- *Fun with Film*—Watch the movie *A Little Princess* together. This sweet story is perfect for an afternoon with someone special.

- *Let's Match!*—Match your special guest in T-shirts fit for a princess—or a queen! Use glittery fabric paint and stick-on jewels. Mom or Grandma can make a shirt that says something like *Queen Bee*—complete with an illustration of a bee wearing a crown. Think of funny sayings to add to your shirt, such as

  If the crown fits, wear it.
  Some days you just feel like a princess.
  All girls are princesses.
  Daddy's (or Grandma's or Mommy's or Grandpa's) Princess
  I'm the princess, my brother is the frog.

  You'll have fun wearing your matching shirts when you go places together!

4

A Flower Princess Tea

Princess Daisy, Princess Rose, Princess Daffodil, Princess Poppy—hold court in the flower kingdom with your very best princess friends. This ultimate garden party gives you the chance to wear your prettiest dress and hat. You can decorate a beautiful table with billowing linens and big bunches of flowers.

You're Invited

Miniature straw hats with rolled-up paper scrolls tied to the rim with a ribbon and little silk flowers will be a big surprise when your lucky guests open their mail! (Mail these fragile invitations in small, padded envelopes available at the post office or your local office supply store.)

Print all of the party information on the scroll, and be sure to request that your guests wear fancy hats and dresses. You might even create a poem or rhyme, such as:

(Your name) is hosting a
Flower Princess Tea.
So out in the garden
We all shall be.
Wear a dress and hat,
A big smile too!
I am looking so forward
To seeing you!

Delightful Decorations

This is the perfect tea to have outdoors, but if you are in the middle of winter and wish for a little spring, a sunny room in the house works as well. Think flowers! Use silk flowers to decorate the chairs. If fresh flowers are available, arrange them in small paper cones lined with plastic baggies and hang the cones on the back of each chair with a ribbon. Using your prettiest handwriting or fun sticker letters, put each girl's name on a cone. A fresh white table-cloth with pale green tissue paper leaves and tissue paper flower petals sprinkled all over will give an instant spring garden feel, no matter what the season!

double stick tape holds plastic baggie

staple closed and ribbon handle

Paint pot and fill with small black beans.

Wrap pen and stem together with florist tape.

Creative Crafts

- *Pretty Posy Pen*—For this fun and useful craft, you'll need a ballpoint pen, green florist's tape, a small flower pot, a bag of small black beans, tempera or acrylic paints, paintbrushes, clear gloss spray, and a single pretty silk flower for each pen. Decorate your flowerpot with paint to match your silk flower. While the paint dries, wrap the silk flower and pen together using the florist's tape. When the pot is dry, spray it with the clear gloss coat. (You'll need to do this step outside with an adult because the spray fumes are very strong.) Fill the dry pot with beans and "plant" your posy pen.

- *Teacup Flower Planter*—It's easy to find an old, chipped teacup that cannot be used for tea anymore. Why not plant a flower in it? Ask your guests to bring an old teacup to the party, or shop your local thrift store for some inexpensive finds.

You'll also need small pebbles, dirt, and a flower without deep roots that grows low to the ground. (A miniature Johnny-jump-up is a good choice.) First, put a layer of pebbles in the teacup, then add a little dirt and plant the flower. Give the flower some water, and then add an old silver teaspoon for a fun touch.

- *Paper Butterflies*—Using the template shown, cut four wings from a piece of two-sided heavy stock scrapbooking paper. Attach together as shown with a brad. Wind some thin copper wire around the brad to make the antenna.

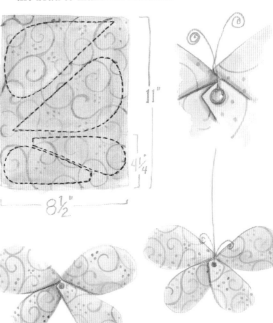

11"

4¼"

8½"

The Tea Table

To continue the elegant flower theme, stack two cake plates on top of each other in the center of the table for teatime treats. Place a pretty tray with a teapot, cups, and saucers on it at one end of the table. Fold napkins to make a pocket that holds several fresh flowers.

A Mouthwatering Menu

- *Puff Pastry Ladybugs and Butterflies*—This treat looks so cute and tastes so good! It's easily made with puff pastry from the freezer section of the grocery store. Roll out the pastry sheet and cut a ladybug shape. Put a drop of cream cheese and jelly in the center and top with another piece of pastry that you "glue" down with water. Make a slit down the center of the back and put holes on each side. Bake until golden brown. The pastry will puff up and look like a ladybug!

3 inch circle

$\dfrac{3}{4}$"

Pineapple and mellon

mellon and banana slice

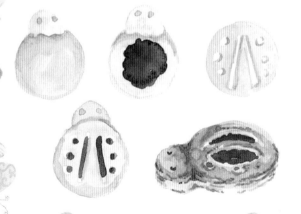

- *Fruit Bouquet*—This beautiful centerpiece is edible too! Use long straws as stems and add cut-up fruit—watermelon, bananas, pineapple, etc. Serve in a pretty, clear glass vase.

- *Oatmeal Shortbread Wedges*—Melt in your mouth shortbread is a guaranteed princess favorite! Bake a simple shortbread recipe, such as the one on the next page, and for a finishing touch, pipe melted chocolate through a pastry bag, making little flowers on each wedge.

Simple Shortbread

1¼ cups all-purpose flour
3 tablespoons granulated sugar
½ cup unsalted butter, cut into small cubes

Combine flour and sugar in a food processor and add the butter a little at a time, pulsing until the mixture resembles coarse crumbs. Form the dough into a ball and knead by hand until completely smooth.

To make shortbread wedges, put the ball of dough on an ungreased cookie sheet and press into an 8-inch circle. Make a decorative scalloped edge all around (you can use fork tines or fingers to pinch dough into a pattern). Cut dough into 16 wedges, but keep them in a circle. Bake in a 325-degree oven for 25 to 30 minutes or until the bottom just starts to brown and center is set.

Cut into wedges again while still warm. Cool on cookie sheet for 5 minutes, and then transfer to wire rack to cool completely.

• *Garden Tea*—Stir up some instant chocolate mint iced tea, or make sun tea if the weather is nice. Sun tea is easy. Simply place some water in a large glass jar or pitcher. Add tea bags. Seal loosely with a lid or plastic wrap and put in the sun until the water is dark. Remove tea bags and pour over ice.

Giggles and Games

"Instant Tea" is something fun to keep on hand for a rainy day—and this type of instant tea isn't the kind you drink! It's a "tea bag" full of fun. Even if the weather outside is stormy, you can get out your supply of Instant Tea for all sorts of party activities. Simply keep the following items in your "tea bag"—

- bandannas or handkerchiefs
- templates of stars, boots, hats, crowns, swimsuits, flip-flops, etc.
- pencils, pads of drawing paper, and construction paper
- beads for making bracelets along with elastic string
- bags of shells found at the craft store
- bags of jewels found at the craft store
- poster board in various colors
- fabric and ribbon scraps
- oven-bakeable polymer clay
- scissors, glue, and tape

Then, see where your creativity takes you!

5.

A Princess Plum Blossom Tea

Let's travel to Japan, a special country where having tea isn't just an afternoon treat with friends—it's a way of life! Tea ceremonies in Japan are known to take several hours, and people still attend special schools to become Tea Masters. You don't have to be a Tea Master to enjoy this tea, though. Just use your imagination and remember—part of being a princess is taking part in and enjoying new customs from all over the world.

Kimono
Template

6½"

4½"

5"

Centerpieces are usually very simple—perhaps one beautiful flower in a vase. Hang paper lanterns around the room. You can find them in different colors and sizes at an import shop, Asian food market, or local variety store.

Creative Crafts

- *Origami Frogs*—Use pretty scrapbooking paper to fold these frogs (see illustration).

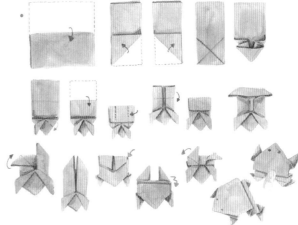

SIDE A

SIDE B

You're Invited

Get your guests in the mood for a Princess Plum Blossom Tea by sending them pretty kimono invitations. A kimono is the traditional robe worn in Japan. These invitations are easy to make using decorative scrapbooking or origami paper, cardstock, and a bit of ribbon. You might want to add a note that guests should remove their shoes when entering the household—a Japanese custom—so please be sure to wear socks.

Delightful Decorations

To set the mood, you must first know that in Japan it is customary to take your tea sitting on cushions at low tables. You can put cushions or pillows around a coffee table to create this effect.

Fun Fans—Make several styles of fans using patterned scrapbooking paper. Use a glue stick to glue two different papers together—you now have a pretty pattern on the front and back. Fold the glued-together sheets of paper like an accordion to make a traditional fan, or cut into a pretty rounded shape and add a wooden stick handle for a different design.

- *Fancy Flip-Flops*—In Japan people wear sandals like flip-flops. Most craft stores have inexpensive plain flip-flops that you can easily decorate with ribbons, flowers, jewelry, or other treasures. Attach these items with a hot glue gun (ask an adult to help you with this step).

The Tea Table

Teapots and teacups in Japan are a little different than the traditional English style many of us are used to. In Japan, the teapot has a handle on the top instead of on the side, and the teacups are smaller with no handles. Try to find a set like this, or at least teacups without handles. Different-shaped plates are fun too! You can find square paper plates in many grocery stores. Cut pretty paper into umbrella shapes for place mats, and fold paper napkins into fans. Let everyone try eating with a set of chopsticks!

A Mouthwatering Menu

- *Simple Sushi*—When you think of Japanese food, you think of sushi, which is traditionally made of white rice and raw fish. Our sushi is a twist on the traditional cucumber tea sandwich—and no raw fish involved!

Simple Sushi

To make a sushi roll, start with a slice of bread, white or whole grain, and roll very flat with a rolling pin. Then, spread on a layer of cream cheese and a little mayonnaise, and after that whatever you choose for the filling. We used cucumber and carrot strips and a little lettuce. Roll the bread up and wrap with a thin strip of lettuce, gluing the lettuce closed with cream cheese.

To make a traditional-looking piece of sushi, start with a slice of white bread, but this time do not roll it. Cut a rectangle and spread it with cream cheese and a little mayonnaise. This will be the rice. Cut a rectangle of cucumber almost the same size. We wrapped ours with some thinly sliced ham placed on the bread. Have fun and be creative!

- *Chocolate Chopsticks*—Dip pretzel sticks in chocolate and then sprinkle with all sorts of treats—nuts, sweetened dried cranberries, coconut, crushed candies, etc.

- *Cranberry-Orange Pinwheel Cookies*—These cookies are so easy to make ahead of time. Roll them in waxed paper, store in the fridge, and then slice and bake. They have a swirly look and a delicious buttery taste.

Cranberry-Orange Pinwheel Cookies
For the dough:
1 cup unsalted butter, softened
1½ cups granulated sugar
½ teaspoon salt
2 eggs
3 cups all-purpose flour

In an electric mixing bowl beat the butter for 30 seconds, and then add the sugar, baking powder, and salt. Scrape the sides often. Beat in the eggs. When the dough forms, remove it from the bowl and divide it in half. Chill for 1 hour.

For the filling:
1 cup fresh cranberries
1 cup pecans
¼ cup brown sugar
1 teaspoon grated orange rind

In a food processor, chop the three ingredients until they are combined. Roll out half the dough and form a 10-inch square. Spread half of the filling over the dough square, leaving 1-inch space from each edge. Roll up the dough, moisten edges, and pinch to seal. Wrap in waxed paper and chill for 4 to 24 hours.

Cut rolls ¼-inch thick and place on an ungreased cookie sheet. Bake in a 375-degree oven for 8 to 10 minutes or until golden brown.

- *Ginger Peach Tea*—Serve hot ginger tea with honey and a slice of peach.

Giggles and Games
- *Japanese Characters*—The letters in the Japanese alphabet are called "characters." Make some cards with simple words—cat, girl, friendship, etc. Make two of each word, leaving the backs plain (or you could glue one design of fancy origami paper to the backs). Cut the cards into equal-sized shapes if they haven't been precut (such as index cards) and voilà! You have a fun memory matching game that will teach you a bit of another language.

| 日光 nikkou sunshine | 友情 yuujou friendship | 心 Kokoro heart | 猫 neko cat | 少女 shoujo girl | 舞 mai dance | 女王 jouou queen | 王女 oujo princess | 王子 ouji prince |

6.

A Sweetheart Princess Sleepytime Tea

Afternoon tea is traditional, but you can have a tea party at any time of day—or night! Sometimes the best teatime isn't in the afternoon! A perfect way to get cozy in the evening is to invite your best girlfriends over for a sleepover. Have everyone put on her jammies, grab a fluffy friend, and settle down for a fun evening with some sleepytime tea.

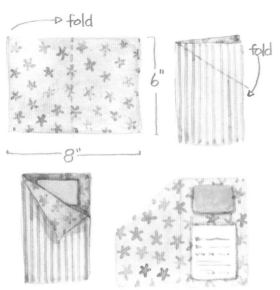

fold

6"

8"

fold

candles (for older girls) and pretty flowers. One fun thing to do when you have guests sleeping over is to put a heart-shaped chocolate on each girl's pillow. That really makes your friend feel like a princess!

Creative Crafts

Get ready for a fashion show for little friends. Fill a box with all sorts of fabric scraps, ribbons, jewels, glitter glue, and have poster board, scissors, glue, and a stapler handy. Now everyone will be able to create a princess fashion statement for her favorite doll or stuffed animal. Take pictures of your creations.

You're Invited

Design your invitations to look like sleeping bags with folded-down corners and crowns peeking out from under the covers. It's easy to make these with two-sided scrapbooking paper and fabric scraps. Be sure to ask your guests to bring their sleeping bags and pillows along with their favorite stuffed animal or doll.

Delightful Decorations

This is a simple party to decorate for because it is the least formal type of tea. Pajamas and sleeping bags are really the main thing. You could decorate a coffee table with

The Tea Table

When you're at a sleepover, you don't necessarily always eat sitting down at the table. Instead, you tend to snack here, there, and everywhere! To make your own portable tea tables, purchase inexpensive wooden trays at a craft store. Decorate them with quick-drying paints or paint pens, and you have instant little tables for all of your guests!

A Mouthwatering Menu

- *Sweetheart Cookies*—Make a sugar cookie recipe and cut the cookies into heart shapes. Bake, and then decorate with icing, candy, and other goodies.

- *Magnificent Meringue*—Make a basic meringue recipe and separate into different bowls, adding a different drop of food coloring to each bowl. Stir color into the meringue and put into pastry bags. Let each girl pipe out fun shapes, her initials, flowers, hearts, and other decorations onto a prepared cookie sheet.

Bake according to the recipe, and then eat up your yummy toasted creations!

Magnificent Meringue

   3 large egg whites
   1/8 teaspoon cream of tartar
   3/4 cups of granulated sugar
   1/2 teaspoon vanilla extract

   In a mixing bowl on high speed, beat egg whites and cream of tartar until soft peaks form when beaters are lifted. Add sugar 2 tablespoons at a time and then the vanilla, continue beating until stiff glossy peaks form when beaters are lifted. Separate into separate bowls and add one drop of food coloring to each bowl. Stir in the color. Put mixture into pastry bag with a large tip. Pipe out designs onto a large cookie sheet lined with parchment paper. Bake in a 200-degree oven for about 2 hours and just beginning to color. Turn oven off but leave meringues in for 1 hour or overnight.

- *Dreamy Drinks*—Serve herbal sleepytime tea with honey at bedtime. Wake up the next morning with hot cocoa served with a peppermint stick or mini marshmallows. A fun option is to put cream in the creamer—which cools down the cocoa and makes it taste a little richer—and mini marshmallows in the sugar bowl. Girls who prefer a more traditional tea party drink can sip English breakfast tea with milk and sugar.

- *Next Morning Muffins*—Add all sorts of goodies—from berries to jelly to peanut butter—to a simple muffin recipe.

Next Morning Muffins

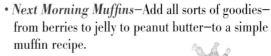

    1¾ cups all-purpose flour
    ⅓ cup of sugar
    2 teaspoons baking powder
    ¼ teaspoon salt
    1 beaten egg
    ¾ cup milk
    ¼ cup cooking oil

In a medium bowl combine the dry ingredients. In a small bowl combine the wet ingredients. Make a well in the center of the dry ingredients and then pour in the wet ingredients. Stir until just combined. At this point add the extra goodies to the recipe, such as chopped apples or pears, mashed bananas, chocolate chips, chopped dried cranberries, blueberries…be creative! Add any spices you might want now also. Spoon batter into paper muffin cups (this recipe makes 12 muffins). Bake in a 400-degree oven for 18 to 20 minutes and then cool on rack for 5 minutes.

Giggles and Games

Make a royal bed for your fluffy friend or doll using a shoebox and fabric scraps. Glue on jewels and design a canopy using the lid of the box. Now you can play slumber party with your cozy companions!

A Little Princess...it's always tea-time...

Lewis Carroll
Alice in Wonderland